ALONE I WAIT

LYNN VANLANDINGHAM

ALONE
I WAIT

NORTHLAND PRESS 1970

LIBRARY OF CONGRESS
CATALOG NUMBER 77–121016

My Wife Nelda

The sound of willow trees
　　rustling in the night
　　　　singing love songs
　　　　　　to only you and me
　　because for all I know
　　　　we're the only ones
　　　　　　listening
　　　　　　to the dark.
The whisper of the passing wind
　　the chirping of the crickets
　　the bell like sound
　　　　of dripping water
　　the call of a lonely bird
　　　　all part
　　　of nature's orchestra
　　　　　playing love songs
　　　　　　to only you and me
　　because for all I know
　　　　we're the only ones
　　　　listening
　　　　to the dark.

Alone I wait –
for I know a tomorrow will come,
    bringing its winds of tranquility
    softening the wrath of life.
            Yes, my darling,
I know the sun
has gone behind the horizon many times
            taking many precious hours
            that might have been ours,
but even now as it sinks
                again to rest
I know a tomorrow will come,
    when again I will glory
    in the light of your presence
            and my love
    as a forgotten seed in winter,
    will burst forth into full bloom
            giving a radiance
    that will lead you into my arms
    and rest in serenity forever.

Time goes so slow
    yet my life runs away
    like a rain-swollen river,
crashing from one bank to the other
    wreaking havoc with all
            in its path,
knowing not what it has destroyed
            to be forgotten
    in the days of its wake.

I saw with wondrous awe
        the sky grow dim
with hovering clouds floating in unison
        to the whims of wind
                as the strains
of violins singing their wistful melodies
                ever rising
        to a full crescendo
                falling gently
        to muted silence
content in beauty
as if fondled by a great musician
        caressing a rapturous chord
regretting the moment it must pass.

Oh, work of life –
How rigorous
and yet
how glorious you have been
to lose only a minute
in lost rhapsody
is a fortune squandered.

The misting fog
   falls sweet against my lips
   gently caressing a fervent soul
      into melodious rapture
   oblivious of the chaos of life
      and then moves silently on.

The sun will rise and
    bring the dawn of another day
    and again a chance
                    to recapture
    the glory
        and need for each other
    the feeling of bliss in knowing
        you are wanted and needed
        every hour of every day.

And so like a lonely tree
                    still standing
    after a terrible storm
    let our love be ever stronger
                    for the turmoils
                    it has seen.

Tomorrow and yet again tomorrow
        that which you hold
                is mine
                to grasp
        and wring from every minute
        the glorious song of life.
I waver on the threshold
        to step forward boldly
        and meet with confidence
the immensity of existence,
                or to thrash
        wildly in frustration
                seeking relief
        in tranquil solitude.

Van Gogh

July 15, 69

Rain drops
hanging by silver threads
from barren twigs,
dark purple
against the hazy sky
shimmer
and drop to the parched earth
rousing old mother nature
into springtime's
laughing tumult
of gaiety.

The rolling countryside
                    quiet
in the wake of a winter storm
                    peaceful
      in its barren rawness
      waiting, ever waiting
            for the wind
          to give it song
               the rain
          to give it laughter
            and the sun
          to give it warmth
               bides its time
          until eternity.

Trees grotesque in their Winter nakedness
silhouetted against the twilight sky
symbolic
as the Sculpture of God
testing their strength
against the erupting wiles of man
and the unrelenting spasms
of ever changing nature.

My eyes
stray to the haunting twilight sky
and my thoughts
wander wistfully
as a waterfall
bouncing over the rocks
touching each with sensual pleasure
in a moment
of fond reminiscence.

The chilling breath of Winter
returns for a last fling of defiance
                    so like
a memory returning to harass the mind
        in annoyance of things long past
        better to have been forgotten.

A piece of wood
torn and twisted by the wind and water
                    lies broken
    half buried in the sand
    there to waste away
                    forgotten
                    yet once defiant
as it lifted spreading wings of branches
                    to the sky
giving shade to a weary traveler
    searching for peace of mind
    wending his way through life
ultimately finding happiness
                    or to end
like the piece of wood
                    drifting
to a lonely shore of sand
                    forgotten
in the wake of eternal life.

The hot sun beats unmercifully
                against my back
                as I labor on.
        Salty perspiration
                trickles down my body
                to evaporate in the air,
                        washing my soul
in a brief respite from oblivion.

Today the zest is gone
　　the love of life
is anchored in the tranquil cove of solitude.
　　The muted sounds of incessant society
　　　　send rippling waves
　　　　against my windows
then lose themselves in the world beyond.
The necessity of self adjustment
in this rigorous scaling of peaks of success
　　is prevalent above all.
　　I must realign myself
　　to the goal I have set
　　　　and begin anew.
No longer can I wait
　　the leaves are falling one by one
　　　　and the winter sun.
　　will come too soon.

A train rumbles
and moves on into the unknown
carrying many loads
gathered along the way.
A submissive mighty force
shuttled hither and yon
by the hand of man.
Symbolic, perhaps,
to each of us
as our journey through life,
our unknown destiny
and ultimate rendezvous.

The lights of the city
Shimmering as stars in
                    the sky
Diamonds flickering in
                the milky way
Each one a dream
                        forgotten
  As the passing of each day
Yet they shine again
    And I smile as
                    I remember
    Each precious
                Souvenir.

Perhaps
one day I shall awake
        to find my soul
    granting my heart's release
    to envelop the wonders of life
        to soothe my brow
        to lift my head
        to throw off
    the chains of society
    and abound with laughter
        as a bubbling brook
            dancing
    from one rock to another
        following its path
        from beginning to end
        not turning back
        but ever seeking
the quiet gentleness of a sleepy lagoon
        coming at last
        to a place of rest.

The rush of traffic
    grows loud with anger
  as the gray still dawn
                creeps steadily
    into full light of day.
No longer does sleep hold me
    for I must grasp each precious moment
      before it slips away
        and is gone into oblivion.

As the shadows of each day hover
and gently settle into dark night
    my thoughts return again
                to those
     I hold most dear
    and caress each precious memory
              for awhile
    my heart leaps with happiness
as I jump from one lost dream
              to another
    recapturing again for a moment
            a glimpse
at this wonderful life in repose.

Life is so generous
   with its burdens and trials
so stingy with its rewards,
      I linger and wonder
what good have I done today
      has my existence had a purpose
or has it been a tribulation to someone
      a yoke around a neck
                  to be cast aside
                  for a lighter load.

Have you ever sat on the side of a hill
    at the break of a new born day
    and listened to the breeze in the grass and the trees
    and watched the animals play.

Have you ever sat by the side of a stream
    and wondered where the water had been
    or where it was going and what it might see
    somewhere beyond the bend.

Have you ever sat in the still of the night
    and listened to the leaves at play
    and pondered your mission in this world all about
    studied the stars – the light of the moon
    and the glow of the milky way.

Have you ever considered
    your life and your goals
    just as the dawn breaks through
    and searched your soul in the evening at dusk
    have you accomplished what you set out to do.

The flickering candle
    caressing the breath of darkening skies
    its shimmering glow
    dances against an amber glass
    arousing sleeping memories.

Night steals on
    and haunting melodies
    flit across the quiet room
    as the enveloping shadows
    hover and gently settle into
    slumbering dreams.

The incessant clatter
    of dishes rattling
    people talking
    music blaring
    creates havoc in the mind of man.

The constant rumble
    of familiar sounds
    causes rebellion and lack of trust,
    makes man cautious
    to do what he must.

Makes him certain
    life is moving too fast
    what should be in the future
    is already past.

No time to sit
    and talk to a friend
    if you don't keep moving
    you've reached the end.

So slow down life
    let's take a rest
    sit here a minute
    now which way's the best.

Soft caressing rays of sunshine
    filter through the clouds
        and soothe the aches
surging about this mass of flesh
    but haunting melodies in my heart
                beat back
like ocean waves washing away the sand
    from a deserted beach
        while the torment of fear
                    stands watching
        like a vulture circling in the sky
        waiting for the last sign of life
to return the beginning again to dust.

Push away the clouds
      I saw a drop of rain
Let the sun shine through
      and drive away
                  the gloom.
      Yesterday
I lost the game
                  I tried
so hard to play
You left me there
            all alone.
with nothing more to say
I walked along
      and wondered then
if I really knew the rules
                  on how to play
the game of love
that's played
      by many fools.

In this wilderness of society
mind of man is constantly besieged
                with impulses
            to betray their souls
            to revert to beast of prey
and scourge the earth
with lackadaisical moments
        of mythical joys.

Leaves burst forth from naked branches
    driving away Winter solitude,
Letting the warmth of Spring
                    give life
    to God's sleeping sculpture.

Not the beginning
                    Nor the end
When I saw you last night
My world came alive
          No cares had I
          Only your youth
As a halo around your head
Glowing in love
          and warmth
Covered my thoughts
As a Willow
          In a rain forest
And I lived again.

I saw the world
                unfold today
        as I watched a flower bloom
                the petals
        opened one by one
                and brushed
                my cares away.

The sparkling dew
                and chirping birds
        an ant went scurrying by,
                my day began
                at early morn
        when the sun
                came through breaking.

A dream ago
   I knew your face
         your smile
   the lingering grace
         of your laughter
         in a crowded room
The night closed in
and in the shadows
         of the darkened room
         we came together
   in a crescendo
               of unharnessed love
   each looking
               for that chord
               of music
   that would make the
               chorus of the world
         a symphony
               in the harmony
               of love.

Loneliness comes like a fog
    stealing about us
hiding the beauty of nature
leading us into unfamiliar paths
    to grope aimlessly
ever seeking that mythical goal of peace
    always out of reach
    and then it lifts
a bit of sunshine comes seeping through
    and we run
like frightened rabbits
    to grasp for a minute
the companionship of reality.

A wisp of smoke
            dancing
        across the twilight sky
caressing the brows of
            sleeping hills,
        lazily cavorting in the evening breeze
            to be forgotten
as it vanishes into eternity.

Silhouetted against the setting sun
            a man
        stoops and brushes away the dust
            and trials
        of another day,
            then disappears
        in the evening shadows
            into eternity.

ALONE I WAIT
has been set in
Weiss and Aldus types
and designed by
Paul E. Weaver, Jr.